T0386035

The Bike Race

Written by
Liz Miles

Illustrated by
Howard McWilliam

In this story:

Jay

Sniffer

Mr Slime   The teacher

There was a BIG hole in
the school roof.

4

"It will cost a lot to fix the roof," said the teacher. "We will have to shut the school."

"Let's have a bike race!" said Jay.
"People will pay a lot to see the race."

"I will stop the bike race," said Mr Slime. "The school will have to shut. Then I can put a hotel there! People will pay a lot to stay in it."

It was the day of the race, but
the bikes were not there!
"The bikes have gone!" said
the teacher.

Then Sniffer saw some tracks.
"Quick! Let's follow them," said Jay.
Jay rode his bike fast.
Sniffer sat at the back.

The tracks led to a rubbish tip.
Jay saw all the bikes in a heap.
Mr Slime had them!

Jay sent a text to the teacher:
Mr Slime has the bikes. They are at the tip. Hurry!

While Jay got the bikes,
Sniffer got Mr Slime.

"We have got our bikes back.
You cannot stop the race now,
Mr Slime!" said Jay.

Back at school,
the race was on!
"3, 2, 1 – GO!"